MEXICO

LETTERS FROM AROUND THE WORLD

Patrick Cunningham

Photographs by Sue Cunningham

CHERRYTREE BOOKS

Distributed in the United States by
Cherrytree Books
1980 Lookout Drive
North Mankato, MN 56001

Library of Congress Cataloging-in-Publication Data
Cunningham, Patrick.
  Mexico / by Patrick Cunningham ; photographs by Sue
Cunningham.
    p.cm. -- (Letters from around the world)
  Includes index.
  ISBN 1-84234-244-4 (alk. paper)
   1. Mexico--Social life and customs--Juvenile literature.
   2. Mexico--Description and travel--Juvenile literature.
   I. Title. II. Series.

F1210.C875 2004
972--dc22

                                    2004041306

First Edition
9 8 7 6 5 4 3 2 1

First published in 2004 by
Evans Brothers Ltd
2A Portman Mansions
Chiltern Street
London W1U 6NR
Copyright © Evans Brothers 2004

Conceived and produced by

Nutshell
MEDIA

www.nutshellmedialtd.co.uk

Editor: Katie Orchard
Design: Mayer Media Ltd
Cartography: Encompass Graphics Ltd
Artwork: Mayer Media Ltd
Consultants: Jeff Stanfield and Anne Spiring

All photographs were taken by Sue Cunningham.

Printed in China

Acknowledgments
The author would like to thank the following for their
help: the Ferrer Cuatepoto family; Sra Mimi Macedo; the
Mexican Tourist Board; and Miguel Cahuantzi Vásquez,
Director of Escola Francisco I Madero.

Cover: Clemente with his cousin, Emma, and his brother,
Abraham.
Title page: Clemente and his friends, Luis and Francisco.
This page: Iztaccihuatl, a volcano near Clemente's home.
Contents page: Clemente with one of his rabbits.
Further information page: Clemente works on a math
booklet.
Index: Clemente's classmates practice their basketball
skills.

Contents

My Country

Tuesday, October 29

Hacienda Ixtafiayuca
Francisco I Madero
Municipio de Mariano Arista
5728
Mexico

Dear Sam,

Buenos Dias! (pronounced "Bwenus deeyas." This means "good day"in Spanish, Mexico's main language.)

My name is Clemente and I'm eight years old. I have two brothers, Abraham and Angel José, and two sisters, Vanessa and Angelica Jasmin. We live near a village called Francisco I Madero, in central Mexico.

I'm glad I can help you with your school project on Mexico.

From
Clemente

I'm in the middle of this photo. Mum and Dad are in the back. In front, from left to right, are Vanessa, Angel José, Angelica Jasmin, and Abraham.

Hundreds of years ago, Mexico was home to great Amerindian civilizations. In 1519, Spanish explorers arrived. For the next 300 years, Mexico was ruled by Spain. Spanish is still spoken by Mexicans today.

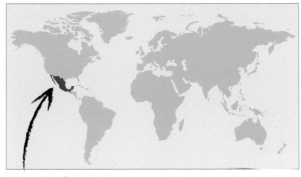

Mexico's place in the world.

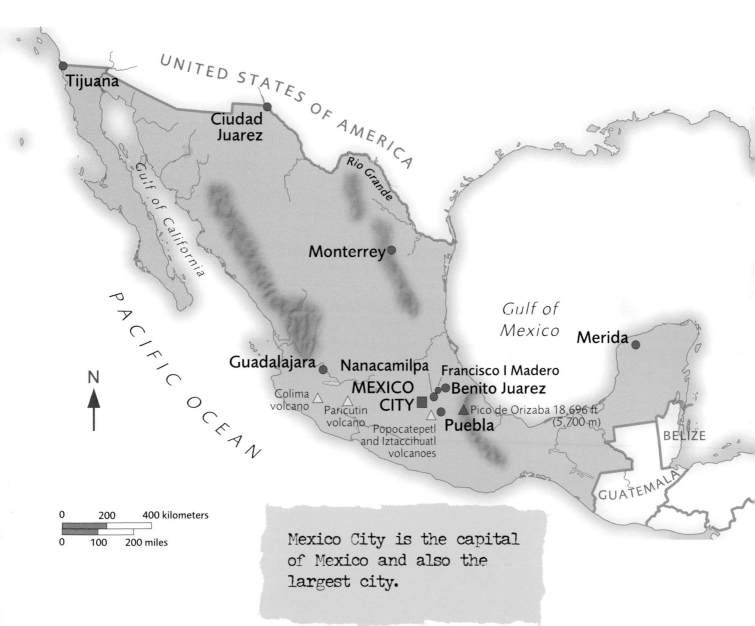

Mexico City is the capital of Mexico and also the largest city.

These farmers are taking their livestock through the streets of Nanacamilpa, to sell them at the market.

Clemente's village is near a town called Nanacamilpa, which is about 4 miles (7 kilometers) away. It is a market town, where local farmers sell their produce.

Most of the land in the area used to belong to rich landowners. They grew mainly *maguey*, a kind of cactus, used to make a drink called *pulque* (pronounced "pull-key").

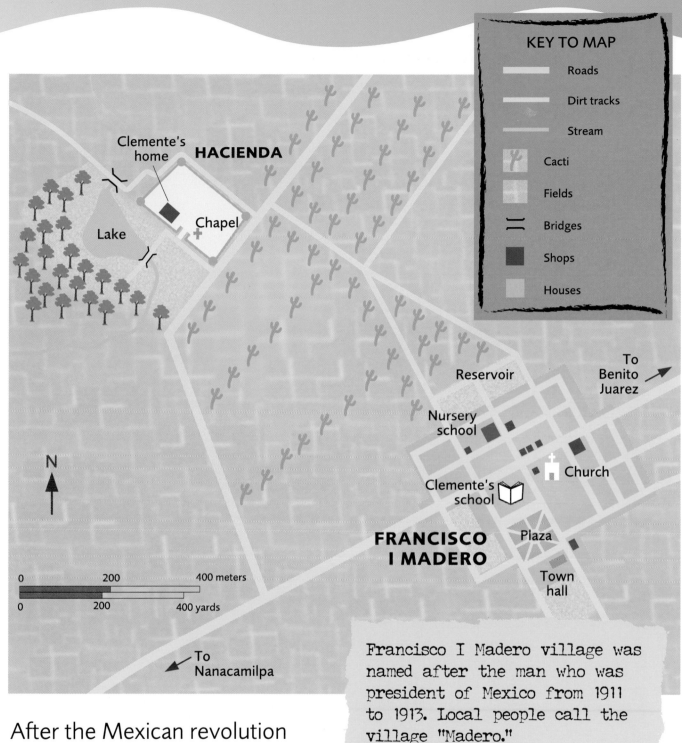

KEY TO MAP

Roads

Dirt tracks

Stream

Cacti

Fields

Bridges

Shops

Houses

Clemente's home

HACIENDA

Chapel

Lake

To Benito Juarez

Reservoir

Nursery school

Clemente's school

Church

FRANCISCO I MADERO

Plaza

Town hall

N

0   200   400 meters

0   200   400 yards

To Nanacamilpa

Francisco I Madero village was named after the man who was president of Mexico from 1911 to 1913. Local people call the village "Madero."

After the Mexican revolution in 1914, the land around Nanacamilpa was given to the poor people. Today there are lots of small farms growing all kinds of food, including corn, melons, beans, and vegetables.

Landscape and Weather

There are two volcanoes near Madero, Clemente's village. Popocatepetl is still active and there is often smoke coming out of it. Iztaccihuatl, which is a bit closer, is extinct.

Iztaccihuatl is only about 33 miles (55 kilometers) away from Clemente's village. He can see the volcano from the hacienda.

The weather in Madero is fairly hot all year round. During the dry season, from October to February, there is little rain. The grass in front of Clemente's home turns yellow. Mexico's coasts have much more rain and are very hot. In the north there are deserts with hardly any rain at all.

Clemente and his cousin, Jaime, sit on a *maguey* cactus. Madero's warm, dry climate is perfect for growing these plants.

Madero's Climate

January

Temperature
68 °F
(20 °C)

Rainfall
0–1 in (8 mm)

July

Temperature
73 °F
(23 °C)

Rainfall
6 in (150 mm)

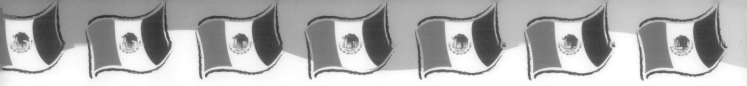

At Home

Clemente lives in a hacienda. This is an old country house that once belonged to a wealthy landowner. When the Spanish came to Mexico, they brought their building styles with them. Haciendas were designed in the traditional Spanish style.

Clemente's family lives in an apartment on the ground floor of the main building.

The hacienda has a grand entrance with high arches. The walls are built of mud bricks, often called adobe bricks. They keep the rooms cool, even in the summer.

In the hacienda grounds, there are many animals, including rabbits, dogs, horses, sheep, chickens, and turkeys. After school, Clemente looks after the sheep.

Clemente is an expert at shearing sheep! The fleece is sold to make wool for knitting and weaving.

Clemente's mother hangs out the laundry in the stable yard. Today there are only a few horses, but in the past there were many more.

11

Clemente's mom gets Angel
José and Angelica Jasmin
ready for an afternoon
nap in the living room.

Clemente's apartment has
three bedrooms, a living
room, a bathroom, and a
kitchen. He shares his
bedroom with his two
brothers. His sisters also
share a room.

Clemente and Abraham play with
a building set on Clemente's bed.
The window has shutters to keep
the room cool in hot weather.

Wednesday, November 20

Hacienda Ixtafiayuca
Francisco I Madero
Municipio de Mariano Arista
5728
Mexico

Oye! (pronounced "oy-ay." It means "Hi.")

Thanks for sending me a picture of your dog. We have two dogs on the hacienda. One of them, Solo, is in trouble because he's been chasing the sheep!

We also have eight big rabbits. One of them has just had babies. I sometimes feed them, but that's really Abraham's job. It's fun to hold the baby ones. They're so soft.

Write back soon.

From

Clemente ↗

Here I am holding one of the rabbits. They live in a shed, but we sometimes let them out into the yard for a run.

13

Food and Mealtimes

Clemente's mom and dad buy most of their food in Nanacamilpa. The town has a market and some stores.

For breakfast, Clemente usually has vegetable soup with beans and *tortillas*. *Tortillas* are small pancakes made from corn flour.

Clemente's mom and dad buy fresh vegetables from the market. The cactus in the front is delicious when it is cooked, but you have to remove the spines first!

Clemente's cousin, Jaime, collects the corn cobs cut by the combine harvester.

Vegetables and corn are grown on the hacienda. Corn is the staple food in Mexico. It is used to make *tortillas* and *tamales*. *Tamales* are corn flour patties cooked in corn leaves. Fried *tortillas* are called *tacos*. They become hard, like potato chips.

Abraham sometimes helps his mom make *tamales*.

Sometimes the family eats outside. Often the weather is very hot, so they prefer to eat indoors where it is cooler.

In Nanacamilpa, the street stands sell all kinds of food. Clemente loves *churros*, which are like long doughnuts.

Clemente usually takes a roll or sandwich to school for lunch. Sometimes he has *tacos* with beans, lettuce, and cheese. For supper he has soup, fried fish or meat, with lentils or beans, and *tortillas*.

Saturday, January 18

Hacienda Ixtafiayuca
Francisco I Madero
Municipio de Mariano Arista
5728
Mexico

Oye Sam!

Here's the Mexican recipe you asked for. It's for tortillas.

You will need: 2 cups corn flour, 1 teaspoon salt, 4 tablespoons margarine, a half cup warm water.

1. Put the flour and salt into a bowl. Rub the margarine into the flour.

2. Mix in the water to make a dough.

3. Knead the dough and divide it up into eight equal-sized balls.

4. Cover them and wait 20 minutes.

5. Use a rolling pin to roll out the balls into thin, flat circles.

6. Ask an adult to help you cook the circles without any oil in a frying pan on a medium heat. When brown spots appear, turn over the circles and cook the other side.

They're delicious!

From
Clemente

We eat tortillas with almost every meal! I love them.

School Day

Clemente's school is not far from the hacienda. Most of the children walk to school. A few who live farther away arrive by car. The school is quite small. Only 260 children go there.

School starts at 8 A.M. and finishes at 1 P.M. There is a half-hour break at 11 A.M. Some children help their parents in the afternoons.

Clemente and Abraham usually ride bikes to school with some friends.

There are 38 children in Clemente's class. This is a geography lesson.

The children study math, geography, Spanish, natural science, history, sports, and citizenship. Clemente learns English after school from a cousin who used to live in the United States.

Clemente works on some questions in his math book.

Clemente's classmates have done a project about recycling. They have made a poster showing how to separate different types of trash.

The school year begins at the end of August, after the two-month summer vacation. There are two-week vacations at Christmas and Easter.

Clemente's favorite class is gym. He is practicing basketball here, but he likes soccer, too.

Monday, February 24

Hacienda Ixtafiayuca
Francisco I Madero
Municipio de Mariano Arista
5728
Mexico

Dear Sam,

Today was Flag Day. Every year on this day we celebrate the year that Mexico gained its independence, in 1917. Each class stood by a Mexican flag. One boy or girl from each class gave a talk to the rest of the school about a president from Mexico's past.

We all marched around the playground and sang our national anthem. Then we had to go back to our ordinary lessons—that was tough!

From

Clemente

The whole school had to stand while we sang the national anthem.

Off to Work

Clemente's dad is the hacienda manager. He runs the small farm and hostel there. He has to spend some of the time in his office, but he likes to get out on the farm.

Here is Clemente's dad on his horse. He always uses his horse to go out into the fields because the dirt tracks are too bumpy for his truck.

These men are using pitchforks to put corn through a combine harvester.

This artist makes a living by selling his paintings to tourists.

In Nanacamilpa, most people have jobs that have something to do with farming. In other parts of Mexico there are big factories making cars and clothes.

Tourism is an important industry in Mexico. Many people work in hotels and restaurants.

Free Time

On weekdays, Clemente does not have much time to play. After school he helps with the work on the hacienda. He likes to spend his time outside.

On weekends, the family usually goes to Nanacamilpa. Sometimes they visit Grandpa and Grandma, who live about 33 miles (55 km) away.

Sometimes Clemente and Angel José like to play on the hacienda's trampoline.

Clemente and Abraham collect marbles, like many children in Mexico. The winner of each game wins the marbles that have been used.

The most popular sport in Mexico is soccer. People all over the country tune in to radios and televisions to follow their team.

Clemente and his family go for a walk in the park in Nanacamilpa.

Religion and Festivals

Most Mexicans are Roman Catholics. One of the biggest festivals is Carnival, in February or March. In many towns there is a parade or display.

In this Carnival parade, the men have dressed up like Spanish *conquistadores*. Some of the costumes are Spanish and others come from Amerindian traditions.

Some Amerindians still worship the gods people worshipped before the time the Spanish *conquistadores* invaded Mexico.

The hacienda has its own Catholic chapel. There is a shrine to Jesus in the main building.

Wednesday, March 12

Hacienda Ixtafiayuca
Francisco I Madero
Municipio de Mariano Arista
5728
Mexico

Hi Sam!

Last week was my birthday. I had a party. All my friends came and Mom made me a cake.

The best bit was the *piñata* game (you say "pin-yata"). The *piñata* is a decorated clay pot full of candies. Each person has to wear a blindfold and try to hit the *piñata* with a stick. When it breaks, all the candies fall out and everyone gets some.

From

Clemente

Here I am trying to hit the *piñata*. Everyone cheers when the *piñata* breaks!

Fact File

Capital City: Mexico City. It is the second-biggest city in the world. More than 18 million people live in Mexico City.

Other Major Cities: Guadalajara, Puebla, Ciudad Juarez, Tijuana, and Monterrey.

Size: 758,246 square miles (1,972,545 km^2).

Population: 98.9 million.

Main Industries: Mexican industries include mining, tourism, food production, motor car and truck assembly, and clothes production.

Flag: The green band on the Mexican flag stands for hope, white stands for purity, and red stands for the blood shed during the revolution. The Mexican coat of arms is in the center.

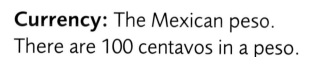

Currency: The Mexican peso. There are 100 centavos in a peso.

Languages: The main language is Spanish. Many Mexican Amerindian people speak their own languages. The most common are Mayan, Nahuatl, and Zapotec.

Volcanoes: The most active volcano is Colima. Other active volcanoes are Popocatepetl and Paricutin.

Longest River: The Rio Grande is 2,000 miles (3,060 km) long. Part of it is also in the United States.

Highest Mountain: Pico de Orizaba 18,696 ft (5,700 m). The mountain is an extinct volcano.

Amerindian People: Amerindians make up about 30 percent of Mexico's population. They are descendants of the Aztecs, Mayans, and other groups who lived in Mexico before the Spanish arrived. Examples of Amerindian architecture can still be seen today, such as the pyramids in this photograph.

Main Religions: Most Mexicans are Roman Catholics. The patron saint of Mexico is the Virgin of Guadalupe. Her saint's day is on December 12. There are also some Protestants and a small number of Jewish people. Some Amerindian people still follow traditional beliefs.

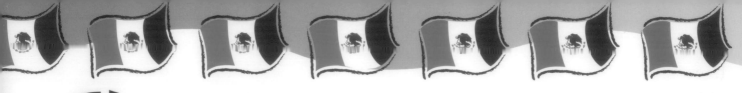

Glossary

adobe bricks Bricks made from mud and dried in the sun.

Amerindians The people who were already living in South America before Spanish explorers found it.

conquistadores The Spanish soldiers who invaded Central and South America in the sixteenth century.

desert A very dry area of land where it does not rain.

extinct A term used to describe a volcano that has not erupted for thousands of years.

fleece The wool from a sheep once it has been cut off.

hacienda The Spanish word for a grand country house and the land around it.

hostel A large house where groups of people can stay for a short time.

independence The freedom of a country to rule its own people, rather than being ruled by a government from another country.

piñata A ceramic pot filled with candies. Children wear blindfolds and hit it with sticks until the pot breaks and the candies fall out.

pulque A low-alcohol drink made from the juice of the maguey cactus.

revolution When the people of a country overthrow their government by force. This usually happens when a government does not allow elections to take place.

shrine A small area set aside for religious worship. It can be on its own or inside a larger church.

staple food Food that makes up an important part of a country's diet.

taco A fried *tortilla*.

tortilla A pancake usually made from corn flour. In Mexico, *tortillas* are eaten with nearly every meal.

volcano A mountain formed when melted rock (lava) comes to the Earth's surface.

Further Information

Information books:

Parker, Edward. *The Changing Face Of Mexico*. Raintree/Steck-Vaughn, 2002.

Ganeri, Anita. *Country Topics: Mexico*. Watts, 1995.

Deary, Terry. *Horrible Histories: The Angry Aztecs and The Incredible Incas*. Scholastic, 2001.

Roop, Peter. *A Visit to Mexico*. Heinemann First Library, 2000.

Richardson, Adele. *Let's Investigate: Mexico*. Creative Education, 1998.

Fiction:

Alarcón, Francisco X. *From the Bellybutton of the Moon*. Children's Book Press,1998.

Geeslin, Campbell. *How Nanita Learned to Make Flan*. Atheneum, 1999.

Joose, B.M. *Ghost Wings*. Chronicle, 2001.

Estes, Kristyn. *Manuela's Gift*. Chronicle, 1999.

Web sites:

Mexican Tourist Board
www.visitmexico.com
Official site of the Mexican tourist board. Lots of information about all parts of Mexico.

Mexico for Kids
www.elbalero.gob.mx/index_kids.html
Mexican government web site with lots of information and fun things to do.

Index

Numbers in **bold** refer to photographs and illustrations.